Recalibrating

Gravity

a memoir

Mary Keating

"A tender, pensive memoir in verse, *Recalibrating Gravity* is so engrossing in its subtleties, that I found myself unwilling to stop reading to take notes. For me, a memorable poem should ask questions I had not considered before reading it. From the first poem in this collection to the last, Keating draws the reader into her own exploration of life's meaning. From life before a car accident at age 15 that permanently changed her life, to all of the cherished and ordinary moments that follow, *Recalibrating Gravity* traverses into our 'temporary existence / more precious than the stars.' Through her consideration of 'the scenes in between,' Keating writes of 'what came and went / and still remains' even as we all 'create chaos out of order.' *Recalibrating Gravity* is impactful, rare, and supple — a book that has stayed with me since I turned the last page."

—**Joan Kwon Glass, author of** *NIGHT SWIM*

"As a general rule, United Spinal Association's member publication, *New Mobility*, does not publish poetry. Yet, when Mary Keating's poem, 'Hospital's Care (a poem about the ER and SCI)' pinged my inbox, I knew we must make an exception. Most of our members are wheelchair users, and *New Mobility* prides itself on centering their authentic experiences, and that's what Keating delivers: Clear-eyed authenticity. Now she's written a book of poetry, *Recalibrating Gravity,* and everyone should read it. It's accessible, witty, and true — yes, it hurts, too, as it evokes empathy and understanding. But it has a warmth that's hard to explain. Perhaps it's the way Keating drops in reminders that as alone as she felt in many of the documented moments, she wasn't. Even when those who ought to have known better catastrophically did not, and engaged in extreme stupidity, the conclusion is that she is here, she is real, she belongs."

—**Josie Byzek, Senior Director, Communications and Digital Experience, United Spinal Association**

"Mary Keating's *Recalibrating Gravity* is a window into the author's world — its triumphs and sadnesses. This book is full of odd things, keenly observed — as in the poems 'Bungaroosh' and 'The Goat of Christmas Past' and so many others."

—Charles Rafferty, Poet

"*Recalibrating Gravity* is a peek into the swirling wheels of joy and laughter, tragedy and triumph, love and blessings in the world of Mary, a poet, a lawyer and an adventurer par excellence. In the end you will find yourself with a new friend who has welcomed your heart into her heart, having a conversation as if you had known each other all along."

—Dr. Karen Shields, Integrative Wellness Clinician

"Punctuated by Mary's beautiful artwork, her memoir written in verse reaches deeper into the psyche than prose alone could aspire to achieve. From the heart-breaking 'Broken Bits,' to the heart-filling, 'A Brief History of Forever,' the strength found in the extraordinary variety of poems in *Recalibrating Gravity* leaves us with a deepened ability to approach our own adversity."

—Katie Dozier, The Poetry Space

"I opened Mary Keating's *Recalibrating Gravity* expecting to read it as a reviewer and instead devoured it. These autobiographical free-verse poems are achingly honest and subversively creative. Mary and I lurk in some of the same poetic venues, so I already knew the quality of her work, but to read her poems as a collection was overwhelming. Her tone more often than not is self-deprecating, but that doesn't hide her ability to cope with challenges and frustrations that I doubt I could handle. A highly recommended read."

—Ed Ahern, International Author and Poet, Editor

Recalibrating Gravity

Mary Keating

woodhall press

Woodhall Press | Norwalk, CT

woodhall press

Woodhall Press, Norwalk, CT 06855
WoodhallPress.com

Cover design: Asha Hossain
Layout artist: LJ Mucci
Editor: Carolyn Keating

Library of Congress Cataloging-in-Publication Data available

ISBN 978-1-960456-15-1   (paper: alk paper)
ISBN 978-1-960456-16-8   (electronic)

First Edition
Distributed by Independent Publishers Group
(800) 888-4741

Printed in the United States of America

To my parents, Liz and Pierson,
who made my life possible.

Photo by Bradford Bachrach, 1952

Preface

grav·i·ty

/gravadē/

noun

1. A fundamental interaction keeping every body down to earth and drawn to each other, counterbalancing the inclination to float away.
2. The prison guard of my paralysis—escaped by full submersion in water, meditation, poetry, or dreams. Also overcome by a shift in perception.
3. Force that lessens as time and space expand between objects and events.
4. Degrees of seriousness lightened by humor.
5. The downward pull of a dog's leash, caused by irresistible smells.
6. Love's invisible glue.

The Making of a New Year's Baby

that might not have succeeded
because my mother wanted to be
a nun or somebody drank too much
or my father never took
the garbage out

with perfect timing
in a universe bearing
13.8 billion years of wiggle room
for me to be the first baby born
in Westchester County in 1958
and win my parents a free year
of diaper service, dinners out,
and a knotted rug

so worn by the time I became
a teenager no prizes survived
except a yellowed front-page article
omitting how my parents
returned before midnight from their neighbors'
New Year's Eve party only to invite everyone over
to our home to babysit my two older sisters
when my mother's water broke and my father broke
the speed limit until stopped
by a policeman wondering
what's the rush?

who upon discovering
escorted my parents
at a pace so slow my father passed
him flashing lights and all
to arrive at the hospital just in time
for my birth certificate to be No. 1

causing strangers throughout
my life to remark it was too bad
my parents lost me
as a tax deduction for 1957
until my father confessed
he had claimed me

causing me to wonder if
my perfect entry cost me
everyone's promised 15 minutes
before my life began

until I calculate the odds of being
on a planet speeding 1,000 miles
per second across billions of light years
but not fast enough
to blur one result:

I am a fucking miracle

The clipping shows a newspaper with partial columns.

Left column fragments:

...urgence.
...re as strong in
...iship with the
...s as any Latin
...ion. The relation-
... Cuba and our
...on Page Seven)

al:

ng Builds
d Cuba

...tches to come
...recent Sunday
...the most im-

...g the article,
...**unsafe to go**
...mas and New
...ectionary ele-

...**phlet print-**
...**y insurrec-**

...**pamphlet, if**
...: the paper's
...ucker's bait
...ganda.
...nost profit-

Wins Prizes in Herald Contest

Keating Baby First in 1958

The winner of the Hera[l] of Westchester's "First Baby" Award is Mary Pierson Ke[at]ing, who weighed in at seven pounds, four-and-a-quarter [ou]nces on New Year's Day, more than an hour ahead of ano[th]er infant named elsewhere as the first born baby of 1958.

The Keating baby was bor[n] at 6:50 A.M. on Jan. 1 a[t] White Plains Hospital and be[comes] the winner of 20 prize[s] awarded by the Herald o[f] Westchester and leading loca[l] merchants.

The beaming parents ar[e] Elizabeth and Pierson Keating 429 Park Av., Rye, who de[clare] they are delighted t[o] have the first baby of the New Year.

The proud pop broke the happy news that mom and the new baby girl were doing fine to their two older girls, Anne Fraser Keating, 2½, and Eliza[beth] beth Thorne Keating, 4.

The girls decided to call the[ir]

So, New Year's day, residents of the entire neighborhood were drinking toasts to the new baby.

The Keatings moved to Westchester only last January and
(Continued on Page Two)

Lady Marine (Ex-Captain) Wins Stripes

Tradition says a M a r i n e Corps Sergeant has to be real tough — but what about pret[t]y Florence Olofson daughter

Right column fragments:

...ing for the New
The Connec[t]
with the section
the New York S
effect on the ra
This is bound t
on the welfare
Westchester con
fic experts decla
The New Hav[en]
already bemoar
muter traffic a
and is making s
subsidies or stat
the lines.
Now, the op
Connecticut. T
trump card in
ers which threa
ally reduce the
York to Bos
freight traffic.
Whereas t
now have ha
antiquated B
with its hun[d]
(Continued o

Did C[...] On Va[...]

The Wes[t]
Board of S[...]
eous indigna[...]
crack which
servants is e[...]

Mary Keating

A Six-Year-Old Girl at Sunday Mass

I'm stuffed into a pew at the Church
of the Resurrection of Our Savior Lord Jesus Christ
with my two older sisters, my baby brother,
my dad and my mother. Our yellow Lab
Heather's stuck home alone. She isn't allowed,
which makes me wonder if she'll be allowed
in Heaven when Jesus comes again.

My sisters and I sport matching yellow
shifts with scenes from Barbados
stitched on in bright threads.
Mom and Dad got them there
last year on their annual vacation.
Mine's really short now and my thighs
are sticking to the wood.

We rushed to 10 o'clock mass.
I barely had time to dress
before Dad yelled: Everyone in the car
in two-and-a-half minutes. I forgot
to put on my underwear.

I hope no one notices
just keeps staring ahead
at my two older sisters
with their shiny blonde hair
not me with dull brown.

I look around and wait
for the priest to tell us
what to do: kneel, stand, kneel,
sit down. If we get it right
we must go to Heaven.

Mom turns and smiles. She's two
sisters away—her beehive hairdo's
caved in on the side she sleeps
despite her silky pillowcase.
I keep waiting for a bee to buzz
out of her hair at any moment—
some miracle to stop

the endless drone. The priest
raises his hands for us all
to stand and my skin smarts
as the wood pulls me back
as if a devil's hiding inside the oak.

I let out a small yelp
which makes me wonder about
Heather home alone
waiting for us—or the milkman—
but it's Sunday and the milkman
isn't coming today. When we stand

my shift rises up. My sister
Anne pulls it down whispering,
"Did you forget something?"
I turn red. She starts to laugh
which isn't allowed in church.

Soon all of us, even Dad,
are trying not to, squeezing
our eyelids, scrunching
our faces, biting our lips,
crying, except, of course,
Mom, mad as a queen bee.

We sit and kneel and stand
in endless repetition and
when Mom's eyes aren't stinging
me, the wood devil is, and I'm secretly
praying Heather won't be allowed
in Heaven because Mom's going
to kill me and I'm going somewhere else.

Jack or Jill

As a child I thought every home
had glass-bottled milk and cases of
Jim Beam delivered weekly
to their doorsteps—though I never
saw anyone ever drink whiskey

Midday my mother stopped
me if I were nearby playing
make-believe to nap in the dark
next to her while she held back
the day's brilliant sunlight with gray
vinyl shades pulled tight against the sill

Quiet and still as death
I'd lie in wait on my father's side
of their king bed—will her breath
to fall into a steady rhythm
Slink off their bed
inch across the floor
out the door to run free
to my motherless Barbies
Bask in the peaking sun
waiting for my two older sisters
to return from school

Other days I'd play outside
for hours unsupervised until
the clang of a copper bell
called me home to a dinner
my mother concocted by coating
fish or meat with Campbell's
soup mixed with Breakstone's
sour cream or Gulden's golden mustard

When my brother arrived
five years later our first
mother's helper came to stay
Strangers living with us every
day fell into our new normal
My mother kept nannies well
past the time she became sober
Long after No-Cal ginger ale
replaced whiskey and milkmen
disappeared into history

Looking back I gather my mother
craved the company of these young
women to keep away a loneliness
a Jim or a Jack could never quench

We were adult children by the time
my mother came out to us, only a few
years before throat cancer tried to
take her voice—then stole her life
after a seven-year battle
But not before she'd gone
back to school and graduated
college, and almost earned
her PhD in theology from Yale

She began her never-
published dissertation
"Marriage and Ambiguity"
while still married
Completed it living
with another woman

I'm older now than she will ever be
Aware secrets almost buried her
alive as she tried to escape
a preordained path while truth
unspoken—hidden—shrouded
kept pushing her to unveil
her magnificence

Her courage still shines
in me—never allowing me
to succumb to the way
it's always been, or worse—
to become invisible

Mary Keating

World's Fair 1964

Throngs of bees vibrating
weave through the Pepsi exhibit
My six-year-old body carried
by the swarm as it undulates
pulling me away from my parents
and my golden-haired older sisters—
all bodies blurring into a mass
of movement

Exiting with droves
out glass doors
into the dark gray sky
An insect sucked along
in the midst of a migration
until the drones disperse
like startled birds

Alone, panic sets in
I frantically scan the crowd—
creep with time like
an inchworm across
the concrete plaza—spin
like a dying top

Lost, wondering who
will take care of me
Fear winds down like a vine
around my body
planting me in place

I'm torn between staying
or tearing myself away
from the pavement
to return inside to the hive
where my family must still be

The sun reappears from behind
an ominous cloud then disappears
quickly chilling a summer day
Just as suddenly my sister
Libby, a burst of sunshine
barrels out the exit doors—
encircles me in her warm embrace

Displacement

My youngest sister's birth
triggered a musical chairs
of bedrooms in our home.
I was the odd person out.

Left adrift to float between
a nursery filled by a newborn
and my former bedroom now occupied
by my younger and only brother,
it never occurred to me to ask
why wasn't he the one displaced.

Back then males simply won
by being males—like getting
the state-of-the-art gym
at Rye High School
while the girls made do with one
from the last turn of a century.

My parents made it seem lucky
to have a choice of two bedrooms
each night. I wasn't fooled as
cartoon menageries or walls
wrapped by red-coated toy soldiers
kept me awake at night.

Mom surprised me a year later
by giving me the bedroom occupied
by Maureen, our English nanny,
the one right next to the kitchen,
just across from the cellar door.

She let me choose my wallpaper—
tiny pink rosebuds for a minuscule room.
She added complementary touches:
a plush pink carpet, frilly white curtains,
a padded white headboard framed by
an inch-wide pink silk ribbon
that ran along a curved light-brown oak
frame matching the color of my hair.

I was so excited to have
a space decorated just for me
it never occurred to me to wonder
if Maureen was just as thrilled with
her new space—the one converted
from the dank dark-paneled office
my dad relinquished—the one he'd
created a few years earlier—steps
from the foot of the basement stairs

—the place we sat and trembled—
when banished by Mom for misbehaving.

Failing Structures

My dad assembled a toy fire tower
in our backyard that overshadowed
the play log cabin he'd made years earlier
We'd climb up to its platform hovering
ten feet above hard dirt with a square hole
cut out for a long thin exit pole

Engaged at play with my siblings
mind absent of potential dangers
I stumbled backwards and tumbled
Landed flat on my back with the wind
knocked out of me so I couldn't utter
a noise or refill my flattened lungs

Lying still, I thought about how my life
was over as my mother scurried to rescue
me—hung her head over mine
as my lips moved like a fish out of water
Then as swiftly as my breath returned
the incident was forgotten—
except by my body

Years later my dad noticed my right
shoulder blade stuck out like a baked
chicken wing as I stood in front
of the mirror glued to my bedroom
closet door admiring my favorite
red-and-blue-striped ribbed top
that clung to every curve

A series of visits to specialists
and x-rays led to diagnoses
of scoliosis and kyphosis
big words a thirteen-year-old
should never have to learn

Only one hour of freedom daily
my body was caged 23/7
in a Milwaukee brace so painful
it dug sores into my sides that still
break down fifty years later

While I slumbered, my rebellious hands
undid the brace's pads and unfastened
its corset's straps with the deftness
of an eager lover undoing a bra
I'd wake to find it lying on the floor
next to my bed in the morning
like a discarded exoskeleton

After being lectured by my renowned NYC
specialist about how my budding
secondary sex organs indicated enough
maturity to handle this sentence
I pulled my bloodied t-shirt up
revealing my open wounds—to him
the hidden ones of no apparent consequence
He finally ordered the contraption remade
admitting his hospital's error

I tried to wear that brace
but my body kept wanting to be
free and I wanted to dance
and do all the things teenagers do
The time I spent in its cage dwindled
until I finally left it in the closet
of my boyfriend's bedroom

My parents stopped asking me
why I wasn't wearing it
Eventually it was swallowed
by a pile of discarded clothes
That's when I began to understand
it becomes easy to ignore something
that doesn't seem to be pressing

Olives

My best friend in junior high loved
green olives as much as I did
After walking home from school
we'd grab a glass jar of cool
ones from the fridge
Run upstairs to my bedroom
Close the door and begin our ritual

We'd pop a plump olive in our mouth
Suck hard until the pimento slipped out
Suck out all the juice—straining
the muscles around our jaws
Flay the olive inside our maws by
scraping the flesh with our incisors
with the precision of a plastic surgeon
Suck again until its skin
rolled paper thin and then
and only then, chew

Revel in the pleasure of pure olive
flavor flooding our tongues

One Christmas my parents wrapped
a can of black pitted olives
and hid it under the tree
When I tore off the shimmering paper
their distinctive tin taste
instantly flooded my mouth

My mother poured the bloated black balls
into a shallow porcelain bowl
reserved for holidays and birthdays
Set our formal dining room table
with my grandmother's fine Irish linens,
Waterford crystal goblets, carved silver,
rose-flowered bone china, steak knives
with antler handles, and the dish
of warm black olives reminiscent of
putrid eyeballs floating in fetid water

I don't think my mother noticed
I never ate a single one

The Ghost Across the Street

When I was eleven my family moved
across the street from a gingerbread house
written up in *Yankee Ghosts*

A portrait artist lived there
with her spouse and the ghost
I never saw her husband

The ghost was born Charlotte M. Peck
but those who knew her called her Lottie

Lottie died at nineteen trapped
by a fire she set to escape her attic room
where her parents kept her
locked up—like all families
in the 1800s when children weren't
quite right—she burned down the house

My affinity to Lottie strengthened
when I became disabled in a car accident
and found myself a curiosity while alive
A teenager locked out
from a once accessible world

My father told me the artist, annoyed by rising
international phone bills, installed a pay phone
to stop her Lottie from calling England
I never wondered how
a ghost that dialed numbers couldn't
just pick up a dime or call collect

Rather, I pondered how
a phantom from the 1800s could find
her dead friend's number in the first place

Which is probably why I learned to see
ghosts as people who just happened
to be dead—not scary spirits

When my father insisted
the only person haunting
that old Victorian was the artist
I realized ghosts also could be
people still alive

But my father mistook who
haunted that gingerbread house
I guess Lottie never
paid him a visit

She was quite a lady
and knew before calling
upon a gentleman she must
ring first—even if dead

Connections

My family's 2.5 acres of paradise
nestled betwixt and between I-95
the Boston Post Road and the train tracks—
a stone's throw from downtown
Rye and the local train station
that my entrepreneur dad walked to
every weekday on a big city career path
from our rambling Dutch colonial
where my stay-at-home mom instructed me
and my siblings to make signs for our first political protest—
an impromptu gathering to stop construction
of a bridge—connecting Rye and Oyster Bay—threatening
Long Island Sound's ecosystem, property values,
and our town's character—proudly carrying
those posters across the Boston Post Road
down through the Ford
dealership parking lot past the police station
onto the southbound platform to rally
with the rest of the town's moms and their budding child
activists—chanting louder than fans in a frenzy
at a Beatles concert

Ban the Bridge! Ban the Bridge!
punctuated by the shake of our makeshift signs
flapping on wooden sticks at the great Moses
who parted a sea of politicians
to build his transportation empire
passing through on a commuter train
to his fiefdom of NYC—not yet enlightened
that his dream bridge would never be built
as rebellion swelled power into the youth
of our town—a town which years later
my property law professor—entrenched
in the privileged-encrusted walls of Yale Law School
would refer to as *that snooty little town of Rye, New York*
when he turned our class's attention to its infamous zoning case—
I wished the floor below my chair would open
and swallow me—until I spotted through the glass door
crude lettering on a posterboard sign taped to the wall
of the hallway and the solidarity
of that childhood moment buttressed me
and I knew it wasn't important where I was from—
only where I was heading

Bungaroosh

The word conveys me to Brighton Beach
England 18th century where men construct
their seaside shelters out of hodgepodge—
broken brick, cobblestone, pebbles, and lime

A temperamental composition
unique to a specific location in time
Prone to crumble if ever subjected
to sustained periods of extreme stress

I imagine the unsung discord suspended
between past and present—strung
between concrete and fantasy—depending
upon a place called home—never sure if

it will be undone by the next deluge or drought
Wonder if I would tap my ruby slippers too readily
when the sky switches melody—resonates me
with the melancholy of something waiting to be lost

Nimbus Clouds Ahead

When I was a child
I couldn't predict
my mother's moods
any better than a weatherman.

Never knew if she'd be
the sweet, soft summer rain
or the pelting, cold
daggers of winter.

Sometimes, when she was
out of her element,
she'd come on like a squall
only to disappear as quickly
back into her cups.

She stopped soaking
us in her toxic liquids
when I was a teenager
allowing me to weather her
with more certainty.

She rarely raged
or drowned me out.
Mostly she dropped
her love like a coat
of dew glistening
on a spring day.

Just before her death
her nimbus changed
from grey to luminescent
then dissipated too soon.

I often find myself
thirsting for any drop
that might assuage her drought.

Love's First Spark

It's been decades since I last laid my eyes
upon his sun-spun hair and deep green eyes
reminiscent of the sea he loved so well.
Our love still haunts my heart. Sometimes
I wonder if he is haunting me now.

We were part of a group of teenagers
off on a two-week house painting excursion
at the lake house of his aunt, far from the familiar
coastal waters that bordered our hometown,
far from parental oversight.

Even though his cousin was my best friend,
we never met until that summer.
I don't remember anything
about painting the house or how we ended up
in a canoe, alone in the middle of a lake
on a star-studded summer
night where the air caressed
our skin with its sweet temperature.
But our first kiss—that memory lingers.

What we talked about before
he first kissed me,
what we talked about afterward,
all those words dissipated long ago
except his question:
"Is it okay if I kiss you?"

I almost laughed.

What teenager asks that before making the big move?
I guess one in the middle of a lake sitting in a tippy canoe
opposite his current attraction. How else
could he explain standing up and walking toward me.
That maneuver isn't done, ever,
without some decent premise. That maneuver will rock
any boat—is destined to rock a canoe—maybe even flip it.

The stillness of that night merged the lake and sky
suspending us in those primordial elements
where I could have hung with him forever.

But excited electrons must keep moving.
We were acrobats on a high-tension wire.
The canoe swayed with our every move,
as we tried to keep our equilibrium—
an impossible feat when passion surges,
sends ripples echoing through eternity.

As he bent to embrace me, he eclipsed the sky.
His eyes replaced the moon and stars—
filled me with electricity as his lips alighted
upon mine like butterfly wings.

Such unexpected delicateness intoxicated me.
I craved his touch with increasing intensity
as his lips flitted on and off mine. My nipples
rose. His mouth, wet and warm,
covered my ear, arousing me
as his tongue and breath moved
down my neck and back to my lips.

29

His tongue entered my mouth
bonding me to him.

We forgot everything.
Time, space, and water.
Oh yes, the water.

As we fell head over heels in love,
we fell head over heels into the lake—
our love baptized in true love's first kiss.

Water did nothing to dampen
love's first spark forever
emblazoned in my mind.

Two

High on an oak limb
four chicks chirping to be fed
One egg smashed below

Salty

I'm a teenager
when an oak cracks
my independence.

Shoulda never gotten
into that Mustang
driven by a boy trying
too hard to be cool
not knowing how
hard his crush would crush.

My beautiful long legs
that wrapped around
my boyfriend never meant
to carry me to another hot rod
to wrap around a tree.

After the accident I'm not smokin'
hot anymore, but strangers still
gawk at me—a wheelchair
now my latest accessory
I can't live without.

Meanwhile, I'm still
hot for sex, frustrated
my wheelchair
cools every cock.

Alone, at a high school party
I just wanna rock. A wannabe
man smokin' a fat cheroot
plops down next to me.

Instead of asking if
I wanna roll, he wraps
his lips around Johnnie
Walker, calls me *fish legs.*

I roll into a mermaid
inhaling oceans that take
a lifetime to exhale.

Paralyzed

My legs, the mutineers,
live out a life sentence
for carrying me
into that Mustang convertible

Trouble is
I'm attached to them

Grace

I don't remember what the police said
happened—how they found me, a teenage girl
screaming to get out of what was left
of a 1965 Mustang convertible caved in
except for where I was sitting

I don't remember crashing into two oaks
I just remember heading for a stone wall
as the teen pushed his car to the limit

I had wanted to get out of that car
a few minutes after I got in
when I realized he was drunk
But he wouldn't let me

I kept praying for a stop sign
or a red light deluded
he'd follow traffic rules
But all lights were green

So it made sense my first words
to the cops were *Let me out of this car*
But I don't remember saying them
Or even talking to the police

God must have touched me between
then and when I came to
Lying at the side of the road
instantly knowing I was paralyzed

How could I not know when it felt
like someone had just slid
a metal sheet into my body
Dividing me at my chest
Splitting my heart in two

Everything below my chest
wasn't just numb
It was like it wasn't even there

And the pain
Oh, the relentless pain
right at the break

God must have touched me then
because I remained so calm

And asked God *Now what?*
For in that moment of forever
God wasn't the stern god of the church
our family visited every Sunday
The one who demanded rituals
that somehow magically saved us—no

God must have touched me
for I felt such love and solace
in that moment of horror
and knew no matter what happened
God was with me—loved me

And God had a plan

Mary Keating

Broken Bits

My accident spun my family's
life upside down—shook
the equilibrium of their globe
but they never let me know it
The middle child—the center of

Mom got the call
rushed to United Hospital
Face above mine she started running
through her children's names
calling them out as always in order
of birth until she reached

The realization it was me
lying there and not another
took her a few minutes to

I was supposed to be safe
at my boyfriend's house
with his mom and dad
Not lying in the ER unable
to move—in agony with

The doctors wouldn't give
me any pain medication because
they feared I had a concussion
They must've never broken
their backs before because

The night is a blur
but a few bits linger
Time moving like a drunk
The nurses not allowing me
to have a watch or a clock
to figure out how fast or how

I'd borrowed my oldest sister's outfit
that night—a silky dark-green top
that matched my eyes—madras pants
I begged the nurses not to cut
as they weren't mine and I'd promised

Barely bearing crushing pain

Unable to move or feel three-quarters of

Whispers of how our one-ambulance
town should've taken me first
instead of the driver whose condition was

Mom finally convincing the doctors
to give me Demerol to try and stop

Drifting in and out of moments

Waking in the freezer of the ICU
my dad sitting next to the bed
his hand through the gap in the rails
holding mine—his other holding
the front page of *The New York Times* to show

His image, a smudge grouped in a line
of other smudges leaning hard to heel a hull
crewing a beauty of a sailboat
in the middle of an oceanic race
he left to be at my side

Telling him I wanted to know how fast
time was passing so he wrapped
his pocket watch around the bedrail
hands nearing 3:30 am and I realized

Bride of Frankenstein

The unwieldy tilt table squeaks as the techs wheel it next to my hospital bed
gingerly transfer my prone body onto it—then strap me in

My PT smiles above me, asks if I'm ready while she angles the table upward
degree by degree into a standing position

But we never get further than a few clicks on a protractor when blood
rushes out of my head to pool at my feet—*go back to zero* written on my face

She drops me to an x-axis then angles me head-down into negative space
Waits for my face to flush to inch me back into positive territory

We advance ten degrees by the end of our session
only after I trick my mind into believing I'm the star

of a horror movie playing the bride of a monster who just wants to be loved
indulging a director struggling to get the scene just to his liking

Forcing me to repeat in an endless loop what is otherwise unbearable

Steps

With an Incomplete Spinal Cord Injury
no one knew what my prognosis would be
I could be up and walking in no time
or only recover bits of function

Rehab became a waiting game buttressed
by Hope buttressed by a Higher Power,
tools and steps of The Program, and my mom
who constantly quipped that at least I wasn't
lying in the Black Hole of Calcutta

Once told the specialists hadn't a clue
I stopped looking to them for my answers
Instead I endured on inspiration
from AA's little black book and slogans
Chanted *Let Go and Let God, Turn Your Life
Over, Don't Project, One Day at a Time*
A Buddhist in training occupying
a bed in Burke Rehabilitation

My mom stopped drinking just in time to coach
her daughter how to walk different steps
through a life of unexpected hardness
I'd no idea what the Black Hole was but
I would never slip into its darkness

Independence Checkup

A bee gets into my parents' bonnet
stings me into going back to rehab
for a checkup before going to college
I resist but they persist

They send me to Rusk in NYC
reputed to be the best
It's summertime and the last
place on earth I want to be

I'm in a wardroom with three
other paras—all newbies but me
I'm independent now—imprisoned
by parental good intentions for a week

A guy on a self-propelled stretcher
invites me up to the rooftop
where he's the goalie along with
another guy healing a backside bedsore

We ride up the elevator
Doors open to clouds of reefer
A group of guys in chairs
slam a puck with hockey sticks

The goalposts lie between the front
wheels of two stretchers with guys
lying stomach down—someone asks me
if I want a hit—I hesitate—then pass

Mary Keating

A cute guy starts flirting with me
Asks why I'm there as he pops a wheelie
Parents satisfies his curiosity
but not before he gets the hots for me

He's a city boy from Rockaway
a world away from my hometown
but only an hour down the highway
Tries to kiss me going down the elevator

By the end of the week he climbs
into my bed late one night
In the morning the nurse flicks
open the privacy curtains—gasps

Sprung from rehab, we visit a few times
He picks me up in his extra-large coupe
My girlfriend comes along with me
Puts my wheelchair in the trunk

His is pinned behind the back seat
the three of us jammed into the front
He whips around a corner onto a busy
road and the passenger door flies open

My friend ejects, head smashing the pavement
Chairs unreachable—we're stuck—
stung by momentary helplessness
Time slows to match her stillness

until she snaps up—laughs and hops
back in—but not back to the same me

44

Passing Time

—0—

Wiggle your toes.
Such an easy act before.
Who would have thought
hours ago
a long, lean, lithe girl
of 15
would have broken so easily.

Well maybe not so easily.
Was it 110 or 120—
whatever the maximum speed
a Mustang could be pushed
when the pedal hit the floor?

Despite her screams
he insisted on showing
just how fast
his baby could go.
He just a boy of 16.

It did go very fast
until an oak,
tall and lean
got in the way.

Maybe he got his wish.
Just before he died
he did break
the speedometer.

—∞—

I know that love of speed—
the way my hair flies
behind me
when racing downhill

How much faster I'd
be dressed
if I let an aide help me.

How much faster I'd
transfer from wheelchair
to shower chair—
from chair to bed—
if my legs let me stand.

But hell—
I can't even
coax my toes to move.

0—∞

With my new van,
I've picked up at least
10 minutes
each way
driving right from
my wheelchair.

I still haven't figured out
the speed of time
50 years after
the accident
crushed T3, T4, T5.

Marking milestones,
when daily tasks seem
to slow me down to zero
while years pass
at the speed of light,
helps me remember:

Graduating law school
Falling in love
Passing the bar
Learning to scuba
Getting married
Cheating cancer.

I don't know when
my journey ends
or how fast I'll get there.

I think my speedometer
is broken.

Hospital's Care

My leg's blown up
All red and scary looking.
It's Sunday.
Solve it at home
I think,
Or I'll have to go
To the ER
And end up caught
In the hospital vortex
That won't spit me out
Again for at least a week
After asking me
Inane questions,
After prodding me
Radiating me with X-rays
Oh, by the way are so much
Safer now and not to
Worry unless you've had
Hundreds.
Oh, you have.
Well
Maybe we can pass on that;
How about an MRI?
Oh, you have a metal rod
In your leg,
Hmmm. Is it titanium?
Don't know?
Can you stand?
No. I didn't see/read your
Chart yet or the intake form

49

Or how you answered
"What can we do
To make it easier for you?"
Here let me just read...
I see you did say you need
Help transferring.
Are you sure you can't stand?

One moment.
Sorry that took so long.
Just a moment.

We're getting some help.
Here, here is the Hoyer lift.
Now we are just going to
Put this under you.
Wait...it must go like this.
No. Hmmm. Let me try,
Just a minute,
I just need to figure out...
No there aren't any aides
That could just lift you.
No, the bed just goes
This low. Sorry.
This lift is no problem;
Here, I've got it now.
Up you go.
Now let me see
How does it move over,
Hmm?
Let's move you over here.

50

No, you don't look like a sack
Of potatoes.
Here we are, almost there.
Oh dear, it seems the battery
Has died;
We don't use this very often
Hmmm.
What? You say
Just raise up the bed?
Oh, that's a good idea.
So sorry.
Didn't mean to
Leave you hanging
There midair.
Like I say we don't do this
Very much.
Now the doctor
Will be in shortly;
Oh, here he is.

Hello I'm the doctor.
How are you?
Before we get
Started let
Me ask you
A few things;
Any pain?
Let me check
Your legs.
Does this hurt?
Whaaaat?
You can't feel.

How long?
This could be serious.
What?
You're a paraplegic?
Oh,
Do you know
How much you weigh?
Can you guess?
No, I don't see what
That has to do
With guessing your
Blood pressure.
No, we don't have
A scale.

What?
The Americans with
Disabilities Act?
I had no idea.
Can you get me a copy?
Really, since 1990?
Wow
Didn't realize it's
Been around so long.

Examining tables too
That lower that far?
Wow!
Then what do you do?
Never heard of a sliding board.
Only 25 dollars!
Really?

Oh yes
Your leg needs
Some pictures.
I'd like to get
An x-ray.
Can you stand?
How about an MRI?
Oh!
That's too bad.

Are you sure
You can't stand?

Mary Keating

Lost Humanity in Wheelchair Dis-Repair

The power drive attached in back of me
moves my chair by Bluetooth technology

It's controlled by a large lollypop
attached by my knee to start or to stop
I spin the dial for speed to excel
Bright lights atop indicate all is well

But beware if those lights stop blinking
A sign technology's not linking
Nothing revives the power that's died
Not a tap or twirl or whack on the side

Any repair to re-engage my ride
depends if it's a weekday: 9 to 5
Insurance pays only for standard workdays
Monopolies causing unconscious delays

Dare I pretend my wheelchair's a car?
I know this ruse won't go very far
in the land of instant auto repair
But my body needs a working wheelchair

Please fix it without a moment's delay
Not in weeks or months or...maybe some day...

Conversations with God

On the other side of forty-nine

Fifty

In addition to a permanent ride
I thought paralysis at fifteen
earned me a lifetime
hall pass

No.

But cancer?

It's a mild one
You'll survive

Fifty-One

You need to rethink
your meaning of *mild*
Neglected to mention I'd lose
my voice for months
after swallowing
that iridescent blue pill
which freaked out my husband
when the Geiger counter jumped
I couldn't be near him or my dogs
for two weeks
How do I explain that to a Lab?

Had to stuff my waste in bags for a month
then wait another before throwing it away

I must glow
in the dead
of night

And now a broken femur—
or should I say shattered

It'll be a piece
of cake—
You'll see
Besides with the metal
rod and pins
you'll be better than new

Fifty-Two

Alright, this is ridiculous
A PT burns a crater
in my ass after decades sitting
in a wheelchair without any serious
pressure sores
My poor body
sewn up, again, like a torn doll
Hope it holds

By the way,
I couldn't feel my flesh cooking
but I feel the nerve
pain afterward. It's relentless
Not even getting the perks
of paralysis
Not thrilled about taking
those opioids either

Just a little setback

Tell that to my law partners
Doubt I'll have
partners much longer

Fifty-Three

Do you think I can survive on my own?

Are you alone?

Fifty-Four

Maybe waiting for me to be
settled in my new practice
before you surrounded
my lungs and heart with a water sack
woulda been a good idea
And that boulder in my kidney?
That was bad enough but hooking me up
with a misogynist urologist
who didn't even know I was still
hospitalized a week after he operated

When I did go home
I had to come right back
because the sadist
screwed up my stone removal surgery
Twice almost killing me
Infecting me with VRE,
resulting in pleurisy and pericarditis
Engaging me in a triathlon to avoid death
Not to mention the prednisone, which keeps
expanding me until my seams might split

When am I busting out
of this hospital anyway?

Oh—and that little white lie
you told me years ago about
surviving thyroid cancer—

I wake up tired
as fuck every day
Do you seriously think
pills can replace a thyroid?

Who thinks up these plots?

They aren't plots
It's just life
It's your life

And why do you still think
I'm responsible for it?

Don't you know by now
Who I am?

Synthetic Hormones

I wonder how much is me—
how much is my medicine?

Cancer wiped out my thyroid
Now my body's regulated
by a guesstimate chosen
from a rainbow of pills
Each color a different dose

Strength cut two weeks ago
when I buzzed about
flirting with anxiety
skirting irritability

Now I'm dragging

Weight gain or loss changes
the amount of hormone
my body demands to survive
Can't lose the heaviness without
extreme effort and when I do

my blood levels are too high
The accountants of medicine
trim numbers as they fight
inflation and the trimmed down
me disappears into new calculations

Weight accumulates like interest but
drains my reserves until I falter again
glancing the edges of depression—
an endless cycle wobbling my moods
like a bobble-headed doll
nodding between balance and instability

while I wonder—who is the real me
and who is the synthetic me?

In God's Hands

Everybody,

in fact the entire
UNIVERSE,

is in
God's hands.

So don't worry so much
I reminded my friend
even though
sometimes I feel
like I'm just h

      a

       n

        g

       i

        n

        g

        on

        to
      Her **fingertips**

about to

f

a

l

l

into

a **dark**

void.

She replied she'd like

to *push*

some   people

o

f

f

.

But I reminded her
they needed instead

to be *pushed* > > > > >
f a r t h e r
into Her palms
for extra <u>**support.**</u>

            IIIIIIIII
The Hubble telescope
recently
discovered what we thought
was a

63

Mary Keating

black void

is really full of zillions
of GALAXIES
gazillions of STARS
bajillions of planets.

Scientists now agree
the UNIVERSE did just appear

after a BIG BANG

and it's been e x p a n d i n g
ever since.

This concept they
can accept even
when atheists
because
they never seem to

venture into the **biggest black hole**
of their theory—

Where did the "stuff"
of the U N I V E R S E
come from
before the v o i d?

To me
the answer has to be...

from God.

And if   God is
holding this   magnificent,
ever-expanding   universe in her
hands, how truly   large and powerful
must her hands   be, but what is
more miraculous
is that they   are also at
the same time   gentle enough
not to bruise   a single butterfly's   wing

Mary Keating

My Mother Around Changed Everything

After compiling my first chapbook
I first thought my mother absent
appeared—only in passing—
in contrast to my father
highlighting my poetry
like the colorful weft threads
of a tapestry ancient

My mother tended to both
my soul and body—especially
after the accident changed
my trajectory's life
from a modern dancer
to an instant paraplegic

She long knew before I did
she must push me harder
or I would never know
the wings of my power—
the ones whose flight
I thought depended
on my run to ability

She stayed beside me
through medical
appointments innumerable
Brought a Big Mac and fries
to an NYU hospital x-ray table
when I craved food comfort

We overlapped our years
college at Manhattanville
as she finished to return
what was youth in her interrupted
Graduated a year before I did

We took theology
classes together pondering
the life of meaning
Laughed until tears as we dissected
the mythic symbols of an Argo
cornstarch box with the dissertation
of a seriousness while concocting
dinner from one of her doctored
Campbell soup recipes

Her humor was so dry I often
would impossible the believed—
like when I was eleven and found
the announcement looking official
her best friend sent seemingly
from the United States government
For a week Mom played along
that our new home's backyard
of two-and-a-half acres near downtown
Rye had been chosen by the Department
of Agriculture for a buffalo preserve

As my mom pursued
her doctorate
I lost her first
to academia
then to her friend
girl turned into lover
then to cancer

I imagined me
of parts still
censured her for
dying and leaving
my world at the early
age of fifty-eight
until I discovered
the presence of her
fullness in every poem

She is my warp—
the life around
which my strength
is woven

Three

**Fire can destroy all
or burn down to the essence
of what lies hidden**

How to Survive in a Wheelchair

Smile.
Until you don't care
what everyone else thinks
always smile—
it protects against pity.

Watch for the smallest
deviations in your path.
If you fail to pay attention,
they will pitch you out
onto the ground
to lie helpless
for what seems like eternity
until you get moving again.

Opt for solid, sensible tires.
Sudden spikes in the road
will have no effect.

Expect your personal space
to be invaded,
especially at airport security
where you will be legally molested.

Prepare for your privacy to be invaded.
Strangers feel entitled to ask you
the most personal of questions.
Make up a few fantastical stories
about why you are in a wheelchair
and practice saying them with a straight face.

Don't worry about what you're wearing.
Wheelchairs have a magical power
to make you invisible
(but be sure to cover your ass).

Treasure those who treat you
like everyone else
instead of as an inspiration
or an inconvenience.

Get used to isolation,
but keep trying to connect.
The world is still learning
the value of inclusion architecture.
Just your presence in it
creates change.

Prepare to confuse.
Ableists will think you have
every disability
and treat you like a child,
or speak loudly and
ever so slowly to you if
they address you at all.

Just don't forget to smile.
Best to be underestimated
and keep the joke to yourself.

Recalibration Toolbox

Always keep handy

PATIENCE—jam extra into tight corners.

HUMOR—WD-40 of life—multi-purpose—spray liberally.

KINDNESS—apply like humor.

ACTION—solvent for discrimination.

DISCERNMENT—energy saver.

FAITH—duct tape substitute, miracle worker.

GRATITUDE—there is no substitute.

HOPE—use when nothing else works.

LOVE—no explanation necessary.

IMAGINATION—everything outside the box.

ACCEPTANCE—when everything else has failed.

Mary Keating

The Wind

As I lie in bed
I hear the wind.
It's whipping outside
tonight, sounding like the sea.
Howling through the cracks
it calls to me—

"Leave your home.
Leave your shell.
Become like me."

I pull the covers tighter
around my soul
damning myself
for not letting go.

Recalibrating Gravity

Fighting the urge
to take up permanent residence
in my bed after yet another
go-round
with this ableist society
I surf the web for an elixir.

I catch a short
YouTube video of
WCMX
disabled athletes united
with their wheelchairs
sporting the skateboard park:
twirling and flipping
defying gravity.

Fearlessly dropping off precipices
they catch air
hurl out of somersaults
fly, crash
pick themselves up
and start all over again
riding high on pure joy.

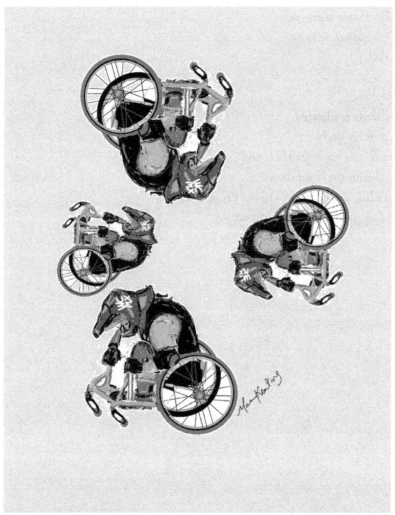

Drawing inspired by WCMX athlete Aaron "Wheelz" Fotheringham

New thoughts
begin to play in my head:
Wheelchair users rock.
Disabled athletes rock.
I rock.

Recharged,
attitude readjusted,
I pull my body
back into my wheelchair and
glide out the front door
heading fearlessly toward the precipices,
riding on the potential of pure joy.

Mary Keating

Wheelchair Dancing

Facing me, my partner holds my hands
Pulls me in my wheelchair to one side
of his legs—pushes me back to center—
Pulls me to the other side—lets go
of my left hand to spin me around

I catch on quickly and soon we are
waltzing across the dance floor
He holds both my hands again
Leans back and spins us like a top
The world becoming a kaleidoscope
Our laughter flying like confetti

Searching for the Perfect Ride
1973–2022

My first wheelchair: a 1950s Cadillac:
oversized, polished chrome, beige upholstery
chosen by my mother to match her Mercedes
Footrests elevated like wings
Fully adjustable
except the seat tilt
Weighed in at 100 lbs

My physical therapist's brilliant idea
to order an adult-sized ride
for a slim teenaged girl
More room for schoolbooks
a winter coat

My brother shined that chair
until its chrome captured every detail
of my junior prom dress

I had it a year

My next chair: compact
not too flashy, black upholstery
some chrome
sized to fit
into more spaces
Half the weight
A faster ride

Senior class Halloween Day
I dressed as a Hell's Angel
My brother fashioned a tailpipe
for my chair out of aluminum foil
that smoked baby powder
whenever I squeezed a turkey
baster attached to a cut-off hose

I rode a sleek blue chair
in law school: black upholstery
No trace of chrome
The frame cracked
the second week
collapsing me inside

Yale's power-plant crew
knew how to weld aluminum
Were so proud I'd never be
swallowed again after fastening
an iron rod inside the cross braces

I didn't have the heart to tell them
Pushed those extra pounds for years

A string of chairs sported rear bars
where friends hopped on
Flew with me down hills
A Brazilian buddy caught
a roller coaster ride in Geneva
while the Swiss watched
with audible frowns

One moonlight summer night
a friend glided me toward Venice's
San Marco square
When the cobblestones blurred below
I twisted around to find him laughing
in the distance as a beautiful Italian boy
whose only English was
My mother is an English teacher
whisked me away

Custom built for a perfect fit
my titanium current chair
purple with magenta highlights
weighs in at only 14 lbs
The finish now
chipped down to silver

I'm the one now overweight—
spilling out of its body

For the first time
in almost 50 years
I'm afraid
I've reached my limits

Mary Keating

A Brief History of Forever

I
We meet in fourth grade at Osborn. You almost catch me
in boys chase girls then girls chase boys.

II
I sit behind you in homeroom at Rye
High, because I'm a K and you're an H.
In ninth grade you move out of town, miss me
being in an infamous car accident the next year.

III
At Manhattanville, I discover you're in my freshman class
working behind the snack bar. You don't seem to mind me
in a wheelchair. You whisk me away
to an evening party in MA while you're manic.
You could be my Prince Charming until
I never want to see your movie-star face again.

IV
Nine years later, fresh out of law school, I tell God
I'm ready to get a husband. I bump into you
browsing records at Caldor's. You take me
to the city—melt me by *The Kiss* at the Met.

V
You keep punctuating we're not boyfriend/girlfriend.
Our bodies punctuate differently
until you disappear with my fairytale dreams.

VI

I get it. You think you can't handle a forever disability.
If I weren't permanently paralyzed, I'd walk away from it too.
Let's not mention your diagnoses.

VII

In Albuquerque, Tom Petty sings to you it's wake-up time.
My phone rings in White Plains, NY. You move across
the US, overfilling my apartment, intertwining our lives.

VIII

Five years engaged, we elope and marry at Sweetheart Rock.
While I'm getting beautified, you commit your vows to memory,
surprise me—as you do for a lifetime—with just how much
you love me.

Mary Keating

Fluid

Somersaulting into liquid space—
a paraplegic plunging into the sea
I venture forth intrepidly

Galaxies whirl by
with every breath
as I dive deeper into the depth

Angelfish curiously stare in my mask—
beckon me join in their play
while butterfly fish glimmer yellows away

Suspended in this watery mix
where diffused sunlight falls
I float down coral walls

Out in the luscious blue
glides a lone eagle ray
capturing my freedom this day

Gravity's prison unlocked for a spell
I forget my limits on shore—
falling to rise—
diving I soar

Bare Necessity

I've got to get into my wheelchair
and go to the store for bread.
The cupboard is so dreadfully bare.
I'm wondering as we lie sick in bed

"How can I go to the store?"
We need to get some nourishment.
We should have made a plan before
we were stuck in this predicament.

We need to get some nourishment.
My husband's usually the one to go
so we aren't in a predicament
when our blood sugar drops so low.

My husband's usually the one to go,
but he's overpowered by the flu.
When our blood sugar's dropped too low,
we're at a loss about what to do.

My husband's overpowered by the flu,
and I'm stuck with him in bed.
We're at a loss about what to do.
How will we ever be fed?

I am stuck with my husband in bed.
The cupboard is so dreadfully bare.
Oh Lord, how will we ever be fed?
I've got to get going in my chair.

Cocoon

Each morning
comforters entice me
to stay underneath them where I'm safe
I know that they're lying
yet still pause

My graduation from Yale Law School with brother David
(Yale undergrad), 1985

Four

Discrimination
Is it its bite or its sting
that stops freedom's breath?

Injustice bites/stings
Sinks its teeth under my skin
I'm armed for the fight

What Makes a Human Human

My classmates scribble
down our law professor's words
as if he's the second coming.
Not me. I close my eyes,
relax in my wheelchair.
Listen as he expands our minds to grasp:
What makes a table a table?
Is it the number of legs? What about a dog?
What if the dog only has three legs?

My body tenses
as it senses
where he's heading.
Eyes wide open when he asks:

"What makes the *handicapped* dog
different than the *real* dog?"

His words slam
into my solar plexus
leaving me cold
cocked, breathless, shocked.
The scribbling scribes don't stop.
Don't pause. Don't see
how these words diminish me.

I can't hear outside my head anymore.
I don't know if anyone answers. The bell
must have rung like it's rung at the end
of every class. The students pack their packs,
drift away just like any other day
while I stay alone with my professor.

I want to cry out.
Call him out.
But my lips are shut—
my lungs deflated.
Familiar choruses rise inside my head:

You are not worthy.
You are not our equal.

I remember:

My high school principal telling me
it was impossible for me to return after my accident;
and when I figured out how, I endured being
stuffed into the stink of the cafeteria elevator
its decomposing slop attaching daily to my wheels.

Living on college campus—I had to go
home to take a shower because the bathrooms
weren't designed with me in mind.

Not one law school dorm room is accessible—
I live segregated across the street.

Relegated to backdoor entries:
barred from buses, boats, subways,
automobiles, trains, airplanes,
bathrooms, banks, bars, stores,
office buildings, restaurants,
hospitals, doctor's offices, dentists—

Every curb, every step, every design
that doesn't acknowledge
my humanity keeps trying to erase me.

They all stem from a thoughtless thought.

The hollow inside my body
becomes the bowl of a bell—
my professor's words that strike
me, the mallet
expounding astounding wrongs
that keep resounding until I crack.

No matter the pain,
the sheer weariness,
my voice must be heard.

I turn sorrow
into a liberty song.

Swelling with each breath—
rising from my depths, soaring
past my lips, I ring out clear and strong:

I am here/   I am real/   I belong

Disabled

I am not just one voice alone. I am one voice among a billion.

It's not a dirty word
It's what I am
It's what a billion are
It's what you will be
if you live
long enough
It may make you
Squirm
Stare
Avert your eyes
Challenge your brain
Fail to imagine
Condescend
Pity
Idolize
Ignore
Tempt to ask
Ask
Race your heart
Confuse it
Break it
Freeze it
Melt it
Sidestep
Walk by
Turn around
Walk away
Or...
Just maybe...
Say it

Handicapped Is My H Word

A triolet

Please stop dancing around the d word
as if you can't just say *disabled*
as if it should go unheard.
Please stop! Dancing around the d word
means your ableism still rages uncured
when you keep a preferred label tabled.
Please! Stop dancing around the d word,
as if you can't. Just say, *Disabled!*

Mary Keating

~~Happily Ever After~~

I am
a princess
alone
in a tower
surrounded
by a moat
on an island
guarded
by a monster

***

Yet I am
no princess
and
there is
no tower
My island
is a wheelchair
the moat and the monster
are the same

***

The loneliness
—the absolute loneliness pervades—

Perspective

What gives rise to hate?
Everything is different
from what we expect.

What gives rise to love?
Everything is different
from what we expect.

Still

how?
how come?
how come
we've
b
e
e
n
to
the moon and back
we   and
can   to
the moon and back on less
find   technology than our cellphones
and still
I sit
a   while
you
way   *g*   sit still
as I sit
n   still
to   *i*   waiting?

start   *v*
m   *o*

Five

**Time's merry-go-round
of holidays and seasons
A bittersweet ride**

Savor Minutes

Time's
   minutes
are treated like
   money's pennies
   by most of us
   unless they fall
   on the quarter hour—
      I'll meet you in fifteen.
      Let's dine at half past.
      Call me at a quarter to.
      Let's go on the hour.
      My father never
      rounded time
      up or down:
Everyone in the car in two-and-a-half minutes. Let's leave in
seventeen minutes. Meet you at four of. Don't ever be
late. He knew the value of every minute,
                  and though
               I found it
            annoying as a
         child that he didn't
         follow convention
         and schedule on the
         quarter hour—as
      an adult I treasure
   all the time he
   let us have
together in
between.

Organic Time Machine

Grapefruit, combined with toast and cup of tea,
conjures up my father, religiously
consuming his Scarsdale diet breakfast—
except he added eggs—jolts of coffee.

Resurrects my grandmother from a box
air-shipped annually—a Floridian
ball of sunshine trumping orange kisses—
Bursting with doses of vitamin C.

Spellbound by this misnomer, a great fruit
halved becomes two crude clock faces without
hands—bends time—toggles me between now and
childhood mornings dining with my dad.

Each dig into pink juicy flesh, squirts, stings,
then baptizes me in bittersweet sprays.

Arrhythmia

My heart races
my breath labors
my body searches
to find the right tempo
even at rest

still.

Requiring 24/7 care now...
my life's rhythm's measured out
in other people's time:
when to wake, when to eat,
when to play, when to breathe

...or pause...

which beats against my parents'
work ethic:
Always be productive...

even when sick.

I know my body
is asking me something
not allowing my heartbeats
to fall into a steady rhythm.

Are you a lawyer
just because your parents said
it would give you the most freedom

...be a solid career choice...

or did you want to be a writer
...an artist...a poet?
Do you still want to be?

Thirty years I've been
ignoring these questions
until my body won't let me.

These are life-and-death questions.
You must choose.

As I write these words
tears drop like soft notes
onto the page
spilling sadness and fear
in a steady rhythm.

That's not the way
I want to live.

I place my hands on my heart.
Feel
for the tempo
to not miss a beat.

For a moment it's there...
like the flutter of a butterfly's wings.

Finite

God clipped my imaginary wings
when I was fifteen
by something as mundane
as a car accident.
Woke me to the predisposition
of the human machine's
operating system. Errors
in perception executed.
Realization time runs down to
zero—a genetic code never
paused. My enlightened self
computes infinity belongs
only to the gods lacking
variable outcomes (running
in endless loops) making
my temporary existence
more precious than the stars.

Mary Keating

Twin Planet

There's a star where all
Earth's memories go

planted in the Milky Way
tucked under Orion's Belt

Far enough to imagine
Close enough to sparkle

I wanted to go there
Live under a different time

An era before a corona
encircled mine

But I fear even light
years aren't far enough

I settle for the stardust
falling from a sister sky

Gathering just enough
to shine through tomorrow

Reflections

When Covid came, I stopped the ruse
advancing age could be concealed.
A lunar glow crept down my head
as a bright sliver waxed into a silver moon.

Luminosity no longer hidden by bottled hues,
I shed threads of moonlight my husband gathers—
presents to me—uncovered treasures
freed from vanity.

Mary Keating

Ouroboros Frayed

Death **is**   out   there--

 a thief   **of light**   waiting   **to** slip

 darkness   **into our**   home; again   we **recoil**

deeper,   **tighter,**   in upon   our**selves**.

Curling until **the**   **tension** becomes   a piano

string about to   SNAP into   **another**

cacophony   as we   long for

a **straight**   line to   before

 a **known**   ending   **was**   devoured,

  before we   must   **turn**   again toward

another loss   **of a**   once   **familiar life**--

 or love, **as**   we keep   hoping to **find**   **our way back**

      to **before**   the beginning   **of the end; before we**
       all broke and   **began slowly**
            u n   **r av**

            e   *l*

                        i

                  n   **g**

106

Six

**Holidays marry
seasons for life, like penguins
But some ditch the snow**

Spring's Flair

Fresh greens peek out
tentatively
until assured then
lose all abandon

Tight buds of yellows, whites,
pinks, and purples
explode—causing even fireworks
to bow down in envy

Bulbs push green shoots
through chocolate dirt
and top them off with delectable hues
devouring the rainbow's spectrum

Each new day the canvas ripens
more expressive than the last
as colors ebb and flow
in an unheard symphony

wrapping all memory
of cold dank days
in a joyous haze

Bees buzz
Birds sing
Lovers swoon

The world hums
wishing all could hold
this pregnant pause
and never yield to Summer

Mary Keating

The Spring Choir

Just before the sun cracks
open an eye toward day
muses etch inspiration
into birds' brains—
like grooves into vinyl

Sparrows warble then pipe
newfound compositions
rousing their human counterparts

Lofty choirs perched on limbs
practice symphonic phrases
over and over and over—excitement
erupts, crescendoes, pauses

A lone cardinal croons

A tufted titmouse tweets tweaks
until the backyard barred owl hoots
signaling satisfaction
with a fledgling song

Later, the moon will steal
her luminosity back
from the sun
Silence will drift
like fresh snow
Muses will fall
back to dreaming

until the sun brushes
the stars from its eyes
again and spins the world
into another day
of possibilities

Mary Keating

Last Summer's Evening

Nestled by the Sound,
Jean and Frank in white
Adirondack chairs,
Me in my wheelchair,
Savored the evening
Spent at the beach.

The waves struck the shore
With a beat more true
Than the band playing
Above us in the bar.

The moon at her fullest
Pulled the sea away
Bedazzling it with diamonds
Cresting on each wave until
The salty sand beckoned
It back to saturate her skin.

Back and forth
Between the moon
And sand
The sea did glide,
Fickle as a young lover,
Caught in a cosmic cycle.

I told my friends,
Throw off your shoes
And dance,
Let the sea and sand and moon
Fill us with music
Beyond our mortal ears.

Throw off your shoes
And dance,
So I can remember the
Feel of cool dark sand
Sifting through my toes.

Throw off your shoes
And dance
So my heart can
Sway with yours.

Was it martinis
Crisp in fluted glasses
Or addictive marlin dip
Or asparagus made with love
That kissed my heart?

Was it the sight of my friends
Dancing free in the night so blue
Among the moon and stars and sea
That reminded me of
Skinny-dipping at the cove
With my teenage love
While sea creatures
Tracked our every move
With phosphorescent light?

Or was it just
Living in the present
With Jean and Frank,
Immersed in the universe,
The smell of salt
And seaweed
Carried on a summer breeze,
That drowned me
In such beauty
My heart danced upon
That beach and
Glided over that glistening sea
To kiss the moon and stars.

The Sweet Melancholy of Autumn

When the air becomes crisp
as an October apple
coloring my cheeks in crimson hues,
leaves mellow into red, orange,
and yellow—
mask decay with colors
of life promising to return
after tree limbs spindle into
skeletons—slumber under icy blankets
of snow's pristine canvas.

Exploding springs push young
greens through tips of old bones.
Death nourishes life. Sunlight stretches
days. Marigolds, roses, cosmos burst—
mirror autumn's complexion reclaimed
from time's habitual strokes.

Comfort rests knowing each fall
will give rise to a fresh beginning.

A Thanksgiving First

The first Thanksgiving
without her husband
was too raw
for gratitude.

She played her part
for her family
coming to dinner.

Eighteen.

I knew that number,
which may have seemed
far too great to some,
was infinity short of one.

When she called
her voice broke.
I knew she couldn't sustain
the act without help.

I wanted to thread
my love through the eye
of her grief and pull
her into tomorrow—
where the first holiday
after his death would be over—

so her tears wouldn't
season the stuffing,
her sadness trim the turkey
or her loneliness echo
in the eighteen empty
crystal champagne glasses
set on her fresh-pressed linens.

But all I could do,
households away,
was send text messages—

tiny lifesavers to buoy her
throughout the day.

Snow

God's delicate lace falls
hushing nature and civilization
like a mother tucking her
children in at night

cold powder coats
black furry noses
as my Labradors dance and twirl
in the freezing blanket
hiding all imperfections

wheelchair tracks paint
abstract art as I
slip and slide
across the driveway
praying I don't get stuck

My eyes take in all the beauty
before plows pull away
the covers and pierce the air
with warning cries
that there are no more excuses
to stay home

Gifts of a Lifetime

It's holiday season again when the world
wraps itself into a glittering present
Christmas carols permeate airways
filling us with peace and longing

for childhood when Santa brought
our heart's desire—sleigh balanced
on slippery sloped rooftops while he
devoured our chocolate-chip cookies
washed them down with snow-white milk

for holiday mornings of sweet treats
ripping open packages carefully wrapped
with love and frilly ribbons streaming
past crisp gold-and-green edges

But now with you gone these images
are a retreating frame of a fabled life—
a bleak black-and-white existence spreading
And I fear it will soon become the all

consuming darkness like the neatly dug
rectangle of the cemetery plot where
you were laid to rest this year
along with hundreds more as we go on

with our debates swirling around gun
control and basic inalienable rights
just like snow—which eventually obscures
even the most unforgiving of sights

Hibernal Solstice

Shadows invade
his lightness of being
when the sun's too lazy
to climb very far
above the horizon

Amid the holidays' twinkle
and sparkle, the night
wraps him into
a cyclical cocoon

where he will barely eat
barely speak
barely answer
his steadfast wife

whose loneliness will flow
into rivers of sorrow
dammed by hope

But even hope can't
hold a constant deluge

When he reemerges
with the energized sun,
he'll have missed her
little bits of heaven—
the moments of happiness
she crafted from emptiness

She won't mention
how her poetry saved
them—each poem
a surrogate sun

Mary Keating

Seasonal Acclimation

Buds

Pop

Colors

Burst open

Fields sway drunk with sex

Life on the verge of becoming

Sun

Beats

Heats up

Bodies bake

Round in Time's fullness

Expanding into golden brown

Fall

Crisps

Summer

Red to brown

Leaves trees silent lines

Arms to gather winter's blankets

Snow

Flakes

Chill bones

Stiff with age

Reluctant to freeze

Succumb to the comfort of sleep

Seven

Motorcycle gang
trapped in the rearview mirror
of Mom's minivan

Making the Grade

A teen's Hail Mary

When my report card blows in by snail mail,
my granny cops the letter from the box.
Should I spill to her why I always fail
or just keep acting like a sneaky fox?

I know when I hear that envelope rip
I'm screwed for sure no matter what I choose.
While Mom and Dad enjoy their summer trip,
she better stay in her lane with bad news.

Perhaps she'll be chill 'bout how I've behaved
like a teenager trying to be cool.
But suddenly I'm woke that I've been saved
when she can't decipher the note from school.

"Angel, tell me the grades for your classes.
Seems I've misplaced those darn reading glasses."

Polar Attraction

She pootled
He tootled
She drank draughts
He ordered naught

She wept for years
He shed no tears
She answered yay
He countered nay

She splayed all outside
He cinched it inside
She was honest as American pie
Everything he said was a lie

They were forever contrary
So they decided to marry
They're happy as happy can be
At least that's what he said to me

The Goat of Christmas Past

Our family fights over such silly
things. But not eating my orgasmic dish?
Who'd have thought bringing a part of Billy
would raise Cain; violate a hostess' wish.

Barred now from every family Christmas,
I serve their sentence of isolation
longing for an ounce of their forgiveness
before this year's merry celebration.

But my sisters persist. I'm the one flawed,
for cooking an exotic meat conceived
to rival any reindeer willy. Blackballed
to dare such a course. Hard to have believed

cooking another member from the farm
raised the old ninnies' prurient alarm.

Mary Keating

Four a.m.

A poem bangs inside to escape my head
"Quiet! You'll stir the prose I just put to bed!"
It settles down for a moment at best
Then erupts like a girl at a slumberfest

"Shush!" I admonish. "You're stealing
my precious sleep!" which forgets
to mention it's worn too deep
to dare to police this petulant poem
running about rampant all on its own

till my mind grabs a hold
knocks it out cold
Revels in a momentary
pause—until a quite contrary

sizzling hot
mystery plot
begins gadding around all frilly and sweet
Starts bebopping with my poetic new feet

They don't stop rockin' and a-rollin'
till the morning rooster's a-crowing
Then—for a few hours—all is quiet
Till my alarm clock begins its daily riot

I stumble about in a morning haze
wondering if I'll ever beat this writing craze

The Poet's Lament

The sunlight beckons me outside
opening jasmines' petals wide
Breezes entice with sweetest smell
as spring's hormones arise and swell
Perched about laurel, oak, and pine
doves sing their arias sublime
Bees draw nectar from luscious rose
as lovers peel each other's clothes
I dream of downy country hills
speckled with cheery daffodils
Apollo warming my pallid skin
Seeping his happiness within
But alas I'm chained to my desk at home
toiling to compose one pastoral poem

Eight

**Dogs bring tears of joy
when they greet you at the door
Heartbreak when they don't**

*Names changed to protect the innocent.

Mary Keating

Dog Lessons

Rye High School, Manhattanville, Yale
abounded with spectacular teachers
Family, friends, colleagues, comedians,
writers, poets, philosophers, theologians
all added to my wisdom as a human
But the sages whose mere presence
shared with me the best biscuits of life
were my two black Labradors
Pumpernickel and Miss Behaving*
who never uttered a single should

The Gift

I hate sending my dog away
when we are traveling.

The moment I first held her,
the softest, sweetest furball,
I already felt her loss,
her time marked by another sun—
seven years to our one—
reminding me to pay
extra attention to each moment.

Stopping to kiss her,
I calm myself with
a few strokes on her fur
magically turning her
upside down
for a tummy rub—

her presence a constant
reminder to embrace life's
small pleasures as
her soulful eyes
speak unconditional love
in between asking
for another Milk Bone.

Mary Keating

A Puppy's Delight

Our puppy's needle-like mouth
nips—more fun than licks—
chews everything from bras
to glass the vacuum missed.

Our grey-muzzled Lab
mellow and sweet
hides in our bedroom
from becoming the next treat.

She yelps as the puppy
finds her savory ear—
attaches to her tasty tail—
forms a caboose to her rear.

We rush to catch
the Labrador train
screeching around
our once peaceful domain.

Dog Gone Howl

you dug me down
and found my bones
then pawed and clawed
until you gnawed
right to my marrow

then filled the mole-
holes with your skunk-
like puppy breath
so I didn't know
the depths you'd sunk

I didn't know
how long you'd been
consuming me

how long
I'd be hollow
with you now

gone

how long
you ferried
how deep you buried

your bones
inside
this brittle heart

137

Mary Keating

Holding On

A life played out in clips

"You can come
and pick her up now,"
the receptionist says
over the phone.

We take the short drive
to the vet's—
shortened further
by my state of mind.

Lately, I can't remember
how I get from
point A to point B.

Ever since Daddy and I left you
at the veterinary hospital
our lives have been playing out
in clips (clip to clip)
with none of the mundane
scenes in between.

I long for all
the mundane scenes
in between—

to hold them
frame by frame
to memorize
memorialize
every moment
from point A
to point B—

from the moment I first
clipped on your leash
(every pull
every strain
every stretch
every smell
every sniff
every stink)
until the moment I let you go.

In the waiting room
the receptionist
passes me your leash
and a bag.
"Here she is,"
she says in a hushed voice.

I grip your leash
for fear you'll slip away—
weigh the bag
in my hands
while Daddy settles the bill.

Is that everything?
There has to be more.
The weight of you
was so much more.

As Daddy hugs me
his tears
flow into mine.
"You can let go
of her leash now,"
he whispers.

But I can't—
because it connects
all our clips
from point A to point B
and tethers us together
for a moment longer
than one lifetime
could ever hold.

Nine

**Love eludes all words
except poetry which holds
it between the lines**

The Ultimate Investment

If you think money's the sole currency
that measures what your life is all about
then you've lost your sense of Time's urgency
and your life may amount to no account

If you think Love is something you can buy
or you'll recapture when your time has passed
you've been bewitched by an accepted lie
and destined to lose all—to finish last

Your life is meant to flow in Love's river
undammed by any thought of its return
It's then you have more than you deliver
and draw beyond what you could ever earn

I hope you recognize the purpose of
your life here—it's to reinvest in Love

The Heart Speaks

We're in the realm of feelings now
misty, murky, mercurial
A mysterious place
where air behaves like water
and earth like fire
Where fortunes align and realign

A place where love is lost
and rediscovered
without a sound uttered

Where something is nothing
and nothing is something

Tread lightly here
Do not mistake emotions
for solid foundations
for they will shift
into another dream

Do not hold onto the spectral spirits
that disturb you in the dark
They have no substance
unless you cling to them
Then they will writhe and bubble
and cause even more trouble—
like coal transforming into fire
instead of diamonds

Against all you've been taught
be vulnerable here
Leave logic behind
along with linear time

And tell—tell those who ask
and those who do not ask—
what came and went
and still remains

Mary Keating

The Kiss

Love's kiss begins
not upon the lips
nor ends
when lovers pull apart
but lands first
within each heart
to pierce,
then thread,
then weave a tapestry—
extending eternity.

A Poet's Heart

true   love
the treasure in   most fairytales
Labrador's kisses   sliming your face
healthcare aides going   to work in a pandemic
parents creating safe nests to surround their children
an athlete's devotion to win gold at the Olympic games
giving your undivided attention for no personal gain
insides of marshmallows heating on a campfire
adult children caring for parents in old age
schoolteachers showing up despite risk
an artist lost in creation of beauty
a dead mouse from your feline
red roses' unfolding bloom
soldiers defending liberty
a baby's first breath
you and me
forever
!

fall

/fôl/

noun
1. The first time the first woman tricked the first man (okay, that's his story).
2. The third season in a cycle of four when leaves blush until they tremble and faint.
3. What people in the winter of life must avoid at all costs.

verb
1. To drop like the stock market, causing some investors to step off their windowsills.
2. To spill, like water pouring, with a passing thought of return, down a ravine.
3. To hopelessly lose your balance when cupid's arrow first pierces your heart.

Transmutation

A contrapuntal poem

With you, I never grow bored
the rock in my river
watching the eddies and haystacks
a place that catches
the boils and widowmakers
random particles
cartwheeling branches like pieces of skeleton
jamming the flow, danger
from a fantastical creature
in a storm-filled day as water rises
piling on granite
a safe haven on a sunny one
until the pressure builds
and though always consistent
overwhelming even stone
in that way, I long for something
shooting from whitewater rapids
that might change reality
churning in a spasmodic dance—
just once for me
mesmerized by utter chaos

Pretension

The damage
at our Italian place
lies equally between us

among the dead soldiers
and the blood-red splotches
on the checkered tablecloth

I wait for you
to take responsibility
for our carnage
But you never do

Without a word
I reach into my purse
feel my virtual power
with eyes never leaving yours

An imperceptible smirk
on your movie-star mouth
makes me retrench

I grab my warpaint instead
excuse myself
with a fading smile

Ready myself
in no man's land
awaiting your charge

Entwined

You breathe me in
I breathe you out.
You catch my breath;
I can't catch mine.

I breathe you in;
You breathe me out.
Our hearts beat once
outside of time.

Our hearts beat twice
and soon entwine;
two souls unite
with love their bind.

Fate tests our love
with earthly fires;
yet love breaks not.
Our souls' desire—

we breathe as one,
our heartbeats too,
for never our love
will trials undo.

I breathe you in
and keep you near—
your heart beats
mine my loving dear.

The Home of Your Life

Today, love your body
Love every damn inch of it
Its folds, curves, and mass

Love its shape
even if no one else does
The skin it's dressed in
no matter the color
no matter how wrinkled
Love its hair or lack of hair
The face it presents to the world

Love what is there
and isn't there

Feel the breath of life
rise and fall into the rhythm
of your heartbeat
But don't
Don't you dare
beat against yourself

There are plenty who will
push you down
to bolster themselves up
You need not support them

There is only one of you
a treasure that can never be
replaced—priceless
Your body is the only home
your mind will ever have

Each morning
Bless it
Embrace it
Love it
Honor it

Hug yourself for me

Bittersweet

The elusive memories of a past love

Trying to remember my first
love's eyes, or mouth, is like searching
for pearls in a cloud-covered sea.

I struggle to pinpoint
what lost me
in those green oceans
or the taste of sweet brine

until I inhale
the summer sun.
Then everything
about him floats
back to me.

Confessions of a Female Siddhartha

A man, magnetic and unscrupulous,
took from me my good fortune and my youth
pretending he was liberating me
in a trattoria where tablecloths
crisscrossed like Catholics before they pray

I was a freshman on my winter break
with dreams of marriage and a better life
away from everyone else's control—
a sheltered girl from a religious house
where natural enjoyments were a sin

While twirling my spaghetti on his spoon
I lost my mind's virginity to lust
believing he was worth my everything
Succumbing to his sexual pursuits
he broke me with such force I almost cracked

Remembering his clawing embraces
I know now I was sleeping while I thought
I was awake experiencing love
convinced he was the savior of my life—
erasing my identity with dreams

When our affair was finally played out
I crawled home to my parents for support
Withdrawing me from college, they sent me
to pray for penance in a priory
where fasting would absolve my mortal sins

155

There I discovered that walls can't protect
me nor religiousness cure all ails
And someone cloistered is still subjected to
seductions and temptations of this world
because our human nature will pervade

Love's antithesis brought me to my knees
My solitude led me far from the world
In meditation I found my true Self
and discovered the path to happiness
where I'm compelled to pass on what I've learned:

When setbacks feel like there is no more hope—
breathe deeply, calm your thoughts, let the love flow
The journey will take you through highs and lows
until you see that everything is one
and you never had anywhere to go

Namaste

Who Will Wake the Sleeping Buddha?

On zombie days when Buddha sleeps
and karma seems to pause,
the world is laid in murky haze
obscuring sacred laws.

On zombie days when Buddha sleeps
the darkness masks as light.
The truth is hidden from the land
and wrongs appear as right.

On zombie days when Buddha sleeps
the Earth is raped for gold
and Gaia is distraught again
despite what we've been told.

On zombie days when Buddha sleeps,
the fortune-monger thrives;
and peddlers pawn their souls for keeps
endangering all our lives.

On zombie days when Buddha sleeps
the leaders tromp and bray.
The people lose true north again
as Love is kept at bay.

On zombie days when Buddha sleeps
should we just close our eyes?
Or should we wake the Buddha now
and stop the streaming lies?

Mary Keating

A Foreign Affair

Every evening
when the offices
are falling asleep
you come—

come with the rumble
of their borne discards,
supplies perched for action.

We smile.
Exchange a few words
allowed by your English
as you refresh my realm—

as you wait to conquer
a new world
and etch your dreams
with a different stroke.

Had I not been you,
an adult in another land
where the children
outshone me
while I struggled
to break past
rudimentary pleasantries
while my philosophies
lay imprisoned
by a foreign tongue—

I too may have thought
you'd never hold
my interest.

But your eyes,
your smile,
the expressions
of your face—

those caught me
long before
you would become
master of my tongue.

And told me
even then
America's stars
would one day
arrest their course

just to hear
the poetry
of your voice.

Mary Keating

The Addict's Wife

Years entombed
by his mistresses
Suspended
she gasps for tomorrow
but only the bones
of their marriage linger
Gathering strength
she cries:

I'm leaving
unless you come back to me
now
for as much as I
love you
I will no longer live
with the loneliness
of one dead
and the sorrow of two living

He begs her:

Don't leave me just yet
I won't be a ghost
forever
I promise tomorrow
I will be better

She falls for him again
Falls like the tears
down her cheeks
She stays
Lies with him
as his tomorrows
consume her forever

Neither living
nor dead
while life waits
for either one
to take the first step

Mary Keating

Chaos — Out of Order

This I know down to my bones
as you create chaos out of order:
I love you. I love you. I love you.
Twenty-four hours back and forth

as you create chaos out of order
trying to empty your basement.
Twenty-four hours back and forth
like a robot gone awry

trying to empty your basement.
Boxes up. Same boxes down—
like a robot gone awry.
Back and forth. Return. Repeat.

Boxes up. Same boxes down.
I worry at the first signs. Get no rest:
Back and forth. Return. Repeat.
You too sense something's amiss.

I worry at the first signs. Get no rest
as you fear spontaneous combustion.
You too sense something's amiss,
like glue left too long in the sun

as you fear spontaneous combustion.
As your brain imprisons your mind—
like glue left too long in the sun—
I didn't know enough before to call

As your brain imprisons your mind,
believing when you say, *I'm okay.*
I didn't know enough before to call
911, always a lifeline—until now.

Wanting to believe that I'm okay,
I won't risk you dying locked in a ward
—911, always a lifeline—until now
as hospitals morph into a pandemic's death row.

I won't risk you dying in a locked ward
while your mind's stuck in an endless loop
as hospitals morph into a pandemic's death row.
I play the serenity prayer in my head

while your mind's stuck in an endless loop
—grasp at your comfort in repetition.
I play the serenity prayer in my head—
ah, but the respite is short.

I grasp your comfort in repetition:
I love you. I love you. I love you.
Ah, but the respite is short.
This—I know down to my bones.

Mary Keating

Insidious

fog penetrates
the cracks
in our foundation
unspooling
across the floorboards
it glides   unnoticed   finds your shoe
slithers   tentacles up your legs
pulling   seeping   flowing
into your pores   into your heart   into your blood
beats   inside
your head
lays obscurity   down
sensing its presence
I hug you tight   will my molecules
to merge with you   my heart
to beat out the intruder
stealing away   our time   together but
the fog keeps on   rolling in bed with you
shades   drawn   I let the fog encase
me   somewhere
deep within
a whisper
of light
flickers

Soulmates in the Confines of Covid

I met my husband when we were amoebas floating in the primordial pond. We didn't have much consciousness then, but I felt him like a summer storm coming. The next time we were together, we were prehistoric flora. Fortune grew us side by side, interlocking our leaves until a dinosaur ate us. We merged in her stomach as acid stripped the memory of lost love. Thousands of years passed before our paths crossed again. We began as seedlings in the pre-Californian forest and matured into magnificent redwoods. Our boughs laced. We held each other tight as the earth shook and the winds howled. Hundreds of years we grew, interwoven from roots to canopy. One day the earth opened below us and pulled our giant bodies down so deep the molten lava scorched and burned us to ash. Our next lives passed quickly as we climbed the tree of life, up the food chain, from bugs to rodents to bunnies to wolves until finally we were snow leopards hiding our glorious furs in virgin snow from the ruthless hunters. We mated often and birthed several cubs. Each year I felt the odds slipping toward the deadly predators until one day my love stopped dead in his tracks as a bullet ripped through his belly into his heart. That bullet killed two snow cats that day. The sorrow of sudden death followed us as we reincarnated into human beings. I don't remember all the lives we lived occupying the top form of evolution. I know they spanned millennia. We existed as hunters and gatherers, nomads, serfs, slaves, kings and queens, teachers and students, brothers and sisters, monks, nuns and priests, and finally as husband and wife. Each human lifetime differed. Sometimes we found each other as infants living in the same household. Other times, we came from different lands or cultures. But eventually we would find each other no matter the distance or deep the disguise. Neither extreme youth nor old age could hide our true relationship—our eternal bond. Sometimes one of us would subsist in a dreamlike state—as if having drunk the waters of Lethe too soon—wed other souls. But always—the other would jar spiritual memory. Once awakened, we'd entwine our bodies as close as physics allowed—past connections tumbling forward into the present—the knowledge of our history stretched across the topmost layer of our subconscious—peeking through the surface like a premonition. Now, we find ourselves in a time of great joy and great sorrow. Trapped together in 2020 AD by a creature as small as we were when our love began, the eternal bond between us pulls beyond its limits.

Time forms an ocean
Spans across eternity
Held by gravity

Poetry Sundae

If love were ice cream
would you serve it before melting?

If happiness were your present
would you accept it?

If grief were disposable
would you keep recycling it?

If sadness were paint
would you choose your own finish?

If anger were optional
would you leave it unchecked?

If friends were tax-deductible
would you ever write them off?

If parents were fine china
would you pick a different set?

If life were so simple
would this poem even exist?

Epilogue

The Journey Home

Course set for true north.
Destined not to veer astray
when earth meets heaven—

crossing over lifetimes, we
enfold back into the stars.

Poems:

"Happily Ever After" (originally published as "Accessible World"), "A Brief History of Forever," "Salty," and "Soulmates in the Time of Covid" originally appeared in *Sixfold*.

"A Six-Year-Old Girl at Sunday Mass" was first published in Robin Barratt's *Family II* poetry anthology.

"Insidious," "A Poet's Heart," and "Ouroboros Frayed" were each nominated for a Pushcart prize by Fairfield Scribes and were first published in *Scribes-MICRO*, which has also published "Bungaroosh," "Hibernal Solstice," "The Goat of Christmas Past," "The Spring Choir," and "The Ultimate Investment."

"Hospital's Care" was first published in *New Mobility* magazine.

"How to Survive in a Wheelchair" was first published in *Wordgathering's* fiftieth issue.

"Last Summer's Evening" was first published in *The Naked Eye* poetry anthology by Poet's Choice.

"What Makes a Human Human" was first published in *Santa Fe Writer's Project*.

Most of the chapter haikus first appeared in *House of Haiku* on Medium and many of my love poems in *P. S. I Love You* on Medium.

"A Six-Year-Old Girl at Sunday Mass" was inspired by my sister and writer, Carolyn Keating.

The "Home of Your Life" was inspired by wheelchair user and yoga instructor, Matthew Sanford.

Photograph credits:

Dedication: Parents' wedding photo by Bradford Bachrach, 1952. Four: Family photo of my brother's and my graduation from Yale, 1985. Eight: Black Labradors, photo by author. Author photo by David Keating.

Illustrations: Mary Keating

Acknowledgments

My life is blessed with so many loving people and angels. My deepest gratitude to all of you who have allowed me to be who I am. You dwell in my heart.

To my parents, Liz and Pierson, who allowed each of their five children to become unique individuals by never holding us back from our creative pursuits.

To my siblings, Libby, Anne, David, and Carolyn, who in each of their ways and with their creativity have made this memoir possible, especially my sister Carolyn, who has spent numerous hours reading and critiquing my poetry, and kindly helped me edit this book.

To Alison McBain, who encouraged me to enter the When Words Count Contest and without whom this book wouldn't exist.

To Steve Eisner and everyone involved in Pitch Week 28, including Alison McBain (again), Peggy Moran, Asha Hossain, and Michael Ketchel, all the coaches (Marilyn Atlas, David LeGere, Christopher Madden, and Steve Rohr), and my fellow contestants, Pamela Martin, Mara Schiffren, and Erik Tolley. I doubt I'd have been the first poetry book to win gold without their generous guidance and insights.

To my publisher, Woodhall Press.

To my discerning readers and dear friends, Karen Shields, Kathy Fogarty, Allison Calomino, Randy Charles Epping, Tina Orsi-Lirot, Jean Wynne, and Ken Bravo, and my fabulous office mates, Wilder Gleason and Donna Chachakis, all of whom help me keep my writing fresh.

To my poetry groups, the Poetry Salon, run by Ed Ahern and Alison McBain, who perhaps are best described as my poetry parents, and MAMPG, run by Mary Anne Case.

To poet Jerry Johnson, who gave me a spot on the Poet's Stage when I first started this journey and continues to generously organize this annual event for poets old and new.

To the open-mic participants of the Hudson Valley Writers Group, run by Bill Buschel, who help my voice continue to develop as a poet, and to Isabelle Engleson, who organized the Westport MoCA's open mic.

To my college professors, especially Sister Cora Brady and Sister Adele Fiske, who introduced me to myths and archetypes, and to my poetry teachers, Charles Rafferty, Joan Kwan Glass, and Britt Gambino, who helped make my poetry shine.

To my first publisher, Josie Bysek from United Spinal, who published "Hospital's Care" when *New Mobility* magazine didn't even publish poetry. I'm so grateful to her and all the publishers after her that allowed my voice to be heard, especially Fairfield Scribes.

To artists Erik Bright, Kiki Sciullo, and my sister Libby, who offered their creative insights, along with Asha Hossain, who created the cover design.

To Dr. Layli Harandi, ND, who keeps my body flexible so I can continue to write.

To Ernie Feleppa, who taught me how to scuba dive, undaunted by my disability.

To my brother-in-law and fellow wheelchair buddy, Martti Miettinen, who has passed on to new adventures.

To all of you I haven't mentioned who have been there for me and have kept me included in life so that I have a life to write about.

To my beautiful labs, who have gone on to play in the Elysian Fields.

Forever and always to Danny, my husband and best friend, who is the breath of my soul. My poetry will always fall short of expressing just how much he means to me.

About the Author

Mary Keating's world turned upside down in 1973 when she became a paraplegic in a car accident at fifteen. Today, she's married, a Yale Law School graduate with her own law firm, an advocate for disability rights, and a scuba diver. A three-time Pushcart nominee, Mary is the Poetry Editor for *ScribesMICRO*. Her poems have appeared in several publications, including *Rattle*, *Wordgathering*, *Poetry for Ukraine*, and *SFWP*. She loves to share her poems at open mics and poetry groups. Mary has served as Chairperson for the Connecticut State Rehabilitation Council and as Vice President of the Rowayton Library. She is a Top Attorney of North America. Mary lives with her husband, Danny, in Rowayton, Connecticut, where they raised two beautiful black Labs from Guiding Eyes for the Blind. More than fifty years after her accident, Mary continues to fight with humor and grace for the ability of the billion disabled people in the world to lead a full and rewarding life.

Author's Note

Thank you for spending the time to get to know me through my poetry.

While most of my poems are autobiographical, some use poetic license to express my observations about life, like "Confessions of a Female Siddhartha." Hopefully, it's obvious which ones are which.

The inspiration to write my memoir in verse came from reading Frank O'Hara's "Personal Poem." I was struck by poetry's ability to hold contradictory ideas and traverse years, sometimes eons, in such a small space.

I love how poems keep changing with each read and how words take on multiple meanings, allowing the reader to dive deeper into the poem—how the form of a poem adds layers of meaning to the words contained inside it.

People are a lot like poems, so it seemed only natural to write about my life in verse—especially since poetry emulates how our mind remembers.

The other reason I wrote my memoir in verse was to show humanity in disability, because to understand its messiness as well as its bliss, sexiness, and beauty, you must feel it. I wanted to break the long-held stereotypes that peg disabled people as either pathetic victims or heroic inspirations. Both labels rob us of our humanity. And hopefully, after getting to know me as a person, you will begin to react as my classmates did in the following situation.

My first year at Yale Law School, I was one of two students who used a wheelchair. The bursar would routinely schedule events in inaccessible rooms unless one of us called and told her we planned to attend.

My second year, my classmates began requesting that the bursar hold events in accessible venues. The first time they asked her about a particular one, she replied, "Why? Is Mary going?"

They replied, "Does it matter?"

Perhaps the most difficult aspect of being disabled is the isolation. I would be thrilled if my memoir helps to open up the world for the billion disabled people in it.

Mary Keating
marykeatingpoet.com